CONTENTS

Introduction ~ 2

M. ~ 3

~ 4

...dence ~ 26

Hope ~ 31

About the Author ~ 36

MAGENTA
YOUR
CONSCIENCE

Inspirational Quotes & Poems
by Hakeem Rahim

ISBN 978-0-692-34895-6, Printed by CreateSpace, An Amazon.com Company
To find out more about Hakeem Rahim please visit HakeemRahim.com

INTRODUCTION

My eyes adjusted quickly to the low lights in the performance studio. I rounded the corner and entered my first poetry event. I was greeted by a deep booming voice: "When you and I tango, winter smiles." Around the room, the audience swayed. The warm studio welcomed me in from the Boston cold. As a freshman at Harvard University, that winter evening of 1999, I fell in love with poetry.

Since then poetry has been an integral part of my life. Although I do not write everyday, I see poetry around me: the way a smile can cry in times of sadness; the way tears can perch delicately on the corners of happiness. I believe we are empowered when we see poetry in our worlds. We all well know our favorite quote, line or verse can shift our moods. In fact, the days we are most swayed by our moods, poetry can swoop in to deliver joy, comfort or inspiration.

The title of this book, *Magenta Your Conscience*, comes from my poem It's not those days. I wrote, *It's Not Those Days,* one morning when I was very depressed, anxious. That morning, my boss called at 7:30 am to check on my arrival time for a meeting. I told him I had the flu. I lied. I was crippled by depression and anxiety, but I felt that he would not understand my debilitated state. I felt I had to hide to mask the shame and stigma of my mental illness.

It's Not Those Days, speaks to the fortitude and disposition we must possess during our toughest moments. This poem reminds me that our response to our worst days is more telling than our response to our best days – adversity not only tests our character, it develops our resilience. On the down days, sometimes rising from bed is the adversity we have overcome. It's not those days is a reminder that sometimes all we have to latch onto is faith, hope, perseverance, confidence, motivation and love.

Magenta Your Conscience, serves as inspiration within the space of adversity. In six sections, I share my original poems and quotes. Each section addresses one of six themes: faith, hope, perseverance, confidence, motivation and love.

I do not pray for the absence of the depressive days. What I do pray for is the strength and perspective to see the why these days exist: to develop strength, resilience and an appreciation of our power-filled days. I pray *Magenta Your Conscience,* can be a bridge, a balance beam and a brick – a bridge to get you over the abysmal days, a beam to support you during down times and a cornerstone for your motivation. *Magenta Your Conscience,* exists precisely for the days that we most need the reminder that now is temporary and faith, hope, perseverance, confidence, motivation and love are eternal.

ACKNOWLEDGEMENTS

Magenta Your Conscience is dedicated to my father, mother, sister, niece, nephew and extended family; to my mentors, young and old, my friends and to my teachers, formal and informal. This book is an acknowledgement of the power of belief, resilience and faith in the things unseen. This book is a physical manifestation of gratitude for everyone with whom I have crossed paths; I thank you each for giving me a piece of experience that in sum total has now allowed me to write a book of original quotes and poems. I thank you, the reader, in advance and pray your grand purpose always illuminates the darkest of your days.

Believe

Believe you can bounce back when your back is against the wall.

Believe you can rise from the ruins.

Believe you can persist when you feel powerless.

Believe you can, believe you can, believe.

Believe you can stand in the sand even when it is quicksand.

Believe you can build bridges
from the bruises by forgive those who forsook you.

Believe you can sing even when you have lost your voice.

Believe you can, believe you can, believe.

Believe you can speak even when the naysayers say you cannot.

Believe you have blessings coming even if you see them not.

And even when you have lost hope, vulnerability and your voice,

Believe you can smile, believe you can sing and believe you can love.

I. Believe. In. You.

QUOTES ABOUT MOTIVATION

The highest mountains are
hills we have not attempted to ascend.
Sometimes we need
perspective

There is a margin of
difference between being
a Vict[im] of your fears and
having Vict[ory] over them.

There are times in life when things can no longer
be shifted, pushed to side, packed in a corner,
hidden under stuff you actually need.
No sometimes in life, like cleaning your house,
you must uproot, throw out, shred, tear up.
For space can be created by exerting the proper
energy. Clean house, clear space, fulfilled life.
Make Room

The clean-up is much harder
than the mess up.
Act mindfully.

I cross the threshold of no
return to sleep to the alchemy
of the night. My only option
bring magic to the day.

Rise swiftly like the speed
of light. Proclaim victory like
the booming speed of sound.
Nature shows all how to be great.

Success is at
your doorstep at the
welcome mat knocking;
are you going to invite
success in your life?

Arise each morning and let
your past tremble in fear.
You are more than a sum of your missteps,
mishaps and mistakes.
You are that worthy conqueror.

Every tree that we chop down
falls somewhere.
We must take responsibility
for our actions.

Grief

Dipped in sorrow's blood,
I'm envied by grief.
And he speaks to me in sideways tongues
Never head on do we meet.
Always stalking me, his disposition never syrupy sweet
For me there is no peace… no sleep

For I must constantly avoid grief,
I must side step him and avoid him,
never allowing him to hold me down or pin me so,
my resistance be a fluctuating existence

Constantly changing,
what I am today, I may not be tomorrow,
so like Evita, don't cry for me Argentina,
and set ablaze to your sorrows,
and scatter the smoldering ashes in the future,
a week from today, six days from tomorrow.

A hole in the center, hollow is pride,
On the surface seemingly full,
Yet it lacks something inside
The core… the essence.
Because of this in your presence I will deceive you,
I will deceive you by performing magic tricks,
Abracadabra, poof!
I will disappear and then reappear before your eyes,
And to your surprise I will stand before you and preach to you true lies.
Strapped to my back and carried with me is an oxymoronic sensibility
I contradict myself and thereby elude predictability

I contradict myself to confuse reality
For reality be driving me insane, the pressures of the world conflicting
with the atmospheric state of my brain,
and while I'm writing each line of this poem, I feel myself about to go insane
but then 39 seconds after that thought, I had an afterthought.

Grief

My consciousness begged me to refrain and hold insanity at bay
So I decided to listen to Miles Davis and John Coltrane,
Painting soul-filled Sketches of Spain
I decided to refrain and learn from two jazz-men
Who know the blues,
Who blow the blues, but never ever manifest or show the blues

See I decided to learn from them.
Their creativity is fueled by their understanding of life
They take heartbreak and translate it into B♭'s and C#'s
They take heartbreak and translate it into B♭'s and C#'s
And through that conversion they master misery,
They master misery they…
Become the masters of misery
and make her submit her heart and her ears
and make misery hear herself being played on a saxophone

And now she can't touch me,
I left misery all alone to despair with despair

So keep playing jazz man,
Keep playing jazz man, Keep playing,
Play the A♭'s and G#'s and all the notes that soothe my heart
And help me to fuel my creativity,
So I can have the strength to leave grief right where I left misery
Have the strength to use your creativity to fuel my creativity

See you resonate with me,
Your jazz like fluidity your brilliance,
My jazz like fluidity my existence

Help me to escape the solemn confines of my mind
That I was sentenced to by misery, help me to create my escape,
help me to create by creating play on jazz man play on
help me to create by playing while I listen to you, grief will have to wait.

FAITH

On This Life: An Ode

On this plane called life,
My spirit flies,
hoovers and dips
Between valleys and hills
Lows and highs.

This life we pilots
All are we,
Controllers of our fate
masters of our destinies
My life a vehicle,
My spirit I guide.

This life we walk on
So many planes,
Accompanied by emotions
All different in name.
Some say smile even when a little down,
Some say dance even with a frown.
I say be, be as you are,
Listen to your self whole,
Be as you are,
Not as others or
Self feel is the goal.

This life, our goal
Is to see it plain,
This life we lead,
Nothing ever in vain.
This life we lead,
love, cry, laugh,

Live.

For when we depart from the sinewy strands
of our bodies, leave the most
elemental parts of our being,
drop the corporeal form that we now know,
we shall be a grand illumination
of our truest selves...

I walk to work in the midst of Pradas,
Stacey Adams and Guccis.
I look down at my feet , broad, smooth, imperfect,
and know I am on the right path.

The city full of Teflon souls, where enlightened be-
ings criss-cross paths everyday...
disciples dodge traffic, prophets post flyers,
Buddhas wait at subway stations...
may we acknowledge the wise beings
we encounter.

Sleep is a beautiful thing.
The armament of the night
has me prepared for the trials of the day.
My revival

Awaken
to that which you are.
Rise.

You can cup hands palms facing upwards
asking for blessings, but your body, soul and spirit
must be ready to receive them.

If you stand in the sunlight of your
convictions, you will never have to shiver
in the shadows of doubt and uncertainty.
Step out of the shadows and
into your conviction.

The greatest act of non-violence
is dropping arms against a soul
that has wronged you.

Seasons

We the seasons do here by proclaim,

Rain, snow and wind storms.

Whereby we bathe you in the suns rays on sunny summer Sundays,

Whereby we bring leaves down in amber autumn colors,

And they fall to the ground in the breeze of the September eve,

Whereby we call forth the Nordic gods to heave swirls of snow and sleet,

Whereby we lay spring showers to wet the breast of callow chicks
resting in their mother's nest

We hereby call forth the souls
of the persons hidden on the limen of the equinoxes

We hereby beckon all these beings to light,

To the warmest parts of the globe

To the curviest part of the Earth

To stand on your individual equators and

Be warmed by the heat of your own being.

We welcome you and to you we present this new season:

Spring

PERSEVERANCE

Nadir

Depression was so real when I was down and doubled over.

I laid on my couch it was a coffin,
It buried all of my dreams.

Lethargy stitched into my brown suede cushions:
I was merely a shade of my brightest self

I lay in silence,
But sleep did not call my name.

My tears danced to the corners of my eyelids,
And slowly dropped towards the ground.

The sounds of hopelessness,
Crept into the crevices of my mind

When there is so much to live for,
how could the lowest point of my life ever convince me of death?

Even in my lowest moments
I had to have faith that resurrection was possible

Hope that my kite could withstand the winds of chaos
Strength to climb from the pit of my fears…

The key to my recovery hung on accepting: I was depressed.

But come what may, I had to rise to my feet,

Because come what may, I had to give up depression's seat,

Because come what may I had to rise and walk

And never, ever give up.

Savor victories for losses will come.
But remember the losses come for you to
be victorious. Be proud of your wins today.

I am a different man today than I was yesterday.
Yesterday I would have laid there, but today
I rose from the grave of my bed to start this day.
You thought you knew, but I am one day stronger.
You thought you knew, but I am one day smarter,
one day more blessed.
I am more than a conqueror.
I am a success story.

Success is etched
in the lines around your eyes.
There is power in your persistence.
You are a champion.
I believe in you.

Living is
Dynamic.
Hard.
Beautiful.
Scary.
But you must.

Tears too are beautiful.

Fall asleep,
dry your eyes,
And wake with renewed conviction.

Dedication is beautiful.

There are blessings in the bruises.
Keep fighting.

Resilience is sexy.

Tempest

Bent not broken,
The poet in me lives
to write another day
to capture the beauty and poetry
in any tempest that almost was.

LOVE

Love

The way your smile cries

In times of profound gladness –

Creasing ever so softly and gently

At precipice of your

Laughter sliding off the side of your face,

Baptizing the ground,

Resurrecting the earth rising

In a new found glory,

Exhilaration only known to those

Who have chewed coca leaves

While ascending the Andes,

It is in those times I notice your beauty.

The way your tears bellow

At the sound of windshield blades

Streaking across dry glass.

Love

(Continued)

Blades questioning the futility of their motion –

The necessity of their existence

Seconds after the storm has subsided,

Its torment coming to fruition,

It is those times that I need you the most.

The way textured heat

Rises from the New York City

Asphalted streets, returning

To the stratosphere from whence

It came like nested sparrows,

In brave tenderness,

Venturing forth to experience its power,

Returning to rejuvenate for another day…

It is then that I want you near me.

Be afraid
not to tell someone that you love them today.
We give so much of ourselves daily but at times we
forget to give the most important thing:
love.

Tell me something
I already know, the
essence of your heart.

Our souls yearn to be
seen clearly.

To my dear free-falling lovers.
Never forget,
Gravity has no weight in love,
Love needs no space in gravity.
Please plunge hard in love's space.

On tons of steel hurtling through dimly lit tunnels,
my heart thinks of you.

When a real man is gentle,
the universe opens
a little wider.

It only takes a moment to make someone's entire
day… offer a compliment today.

The wind from his lips
Like notes, wrapped and
Gently and placed,
In treble clefts of her ears.

Today,
love yourself
even more than you did
yesterday

Imprints

Woman you…
Woman you have touched my soul
And have imprinted your imprints
On my spirit.

I sincerely hope that I can
Wade in your waters
And wonder through your forests.
I sincerely hope I can blow
warm winds
Into the sails of your possibility.

For you,
I seize the salt in the sea
And mix the extracts in the river
To confuse mother-nature
And make her wonder,
"What has gripped that
boy's heart so
To make him do such mind
boggling things."

For you,
I teach time
To double-dutch backwards
And then hop-scotch forward,
So he'll be prancing in circles
And we'll be able to mingle
In this beautiful moment forever.

Imprints

(Continued)

For you,
I tell clouds of cumulous nimbus'
To form in the formation of
school buses
And carry your precipitation away,

For some how,
When I'm with you,
The sun always seems shine,

You are divine,
Heavenly,
Cherubim angels
Pluck peaceful chords
On harpsichords whose notes
Were fashioned by you.

Alpha frequencies forget their phases
And form beta waves
When they bounce off
your heartbeats,
Shattering amplitudes
And breaking confused attitudes,

Unknowingly,
We are one.
Unknowingly
I did not know,

That until yesterday,
Woman you have touch my soul

Confidence

Allow your abundance to flow like powerful rivers
And your giving spirit like the mighty Victoria Falls.
Allow your generosity to seep into hate-filled crevices
And smooth over rough patches of malice and indignation.
You are like mighty waters,
formed but formless
Powerful yet pliant
Yes, you are.

Why be anything less than your beautiful self?

There are always echoes
of your greatness,
embers of your truest self, burning in the places
you least expect.

May your hands be
the tools to emancipate humanity.
May your tongue be the sword to severe malice,
And your mind by the most potent weapon
You will ever have to use to inoculate hate.

Be outstanding with no remorse. Let the silence
cheer for you even when no one else does.
You are your biggest cheerleader.

If you stand in the sunlight of your
convictions, you will never have to shiver in the
shadows of doubt and uncertainty. Step out of the
shadows and into your conviction.

Daily you can choose
success as it lays on the other end of each choice
you make. There is no such thing as failure,
only lack of belief that each second of each day,
you have the power to empower your life.

Your soul is the steady center of the lake;
the shifting winds across the waters move you not.

This you, you only get to do it once,
so do it well, in this life.

Father

With his father across a small swath of water, the young boy was told to jump.
He was learning to swim yet he couldn't understand
why he had to jump in the water to learn,
why couldn't his dad just taken him into the water with him?

"Jump!" His dad yelled. Without thinking anymore the boy leapt flaying his arms,
and then hit the water with a huge splash. Scared, he tread water for a bit and then grab on to his father.
When he looked back he was a good 20 feet from where he started.
His father grab him; the boy heaved a sigh of relief; they treaded back to the small dingy.

The boy asked his father, "Dad, why did I have to jump into the water, couldn't I have just started in it with you?"
His father looked at him gently, but as he always did, spoke with a firm voice,
"Son the first parts of swimming are conquering fear, belief and faith. If I brought you in the water with me,
you would have never had to conquer your fear
of being underwater, yes you had to jump. If you didn't flay,
you wouldn't have had the belief that you could compose yourself once you hit the water.
If I held onto you before you started, you wouldn't have been able to faith that you could swim,
20 feet before I even touched you.
Learning to swim is living life. You must take a leap before you can
truly believe you can do it."

He would always love his father.

HOPE

N.ew Y.ears Manifesto I:

Cry knowing that the sun will dry your tears,

Laugh knowing that the sounds will lighten cherubs ears.

Eat marveling at the riches provided by the earth,

Walk understanding that you were perfection at birth.

Give and forget the cost of what you gave.

Love and forget the price paid.

Remember souls have laid the path before you,

Live, really live, and they will smile from heaven adoring you.

QUOTES ABOUT HOPE

Walk into your greatest self smiling.

Shoot for the heavens and
catch everything in between.

Sometimes mustering
a smile is life's greatest
victory.

Father, let rain, sleet, hail nor snow prevent the
delivery of that which you invested in me: passion.
You have called many and all are chosen to live
lives that are worthy of legacy, of joy, of passion.

Live passionate today,
live your passion, today.

Passed a car with a bump sticker that read
"I HAD Cancer."
The beauty in powerful things...

When you feel the ground shifting under you,
and you can't stand on your own...
know that faith moves mountains
and be still in that knowledge.

Touched souls
Teach souls
To live.

Just because we fail does not make us a failure.
We have more depth than one action,
more breadth than one loss.
Stand in your sunlight.

Even if the sun does not rise
through the rain clouds, my spirit will.
My soul is burning alight with passion,
my conscience
overflowing with purpose.

It's Not Those Days

It's not the days when you leap out of the bed ready to leap buildings in one bound.
Or the days when the roses smell sweet and the honey tastes good.
It's not the days when faith chills
By your right and perseverance is walking in sync step.

Better Yet it is not the Happy Days,
It is the days where motivation has fallen by the wayside, and languish is
The brutal precipitation.
It is the days when you feel to do little and there is much to be done
The days that test your faith, your love and your compassion.
The days where your confidence is compromised
And your esteem is mauled by the abyss.

It is then when the depth of your humanity is tested.
When you have to reach down to reach the gristle,
When you cannot listen to the naysayers including
You own dissenting voice.
That is when you show your essence.

See faith is easy from the armchair,
But when you must fight from the frontlines
Of a dissenting self and win, and come out positive,
Bruises and all, that is when you have showed your
True character and colors.

So today,
I want you paint the town red and blue with me,
Hoist oranges and mauves above your head with me,
Yellow the tar and indigo the ground with me.
Carry stained glass urns full
Of aqua ashes and spread them over
Crystal clear seas of humanity walking
Through train stations.
Magenta your conscience and erase your ego

As today I must do the same.

ABOUT THE AUTHOR

My journey with bipolar disorder began in 1998 when I had my first anxiety attack at the beginning of my freshman year at Harvard University. During that terrifying experience – heart palpitations, sweaty palms and spinning room – I did not know to call it a panic attack, all I knew was it was frightening.

Over the course of this 16+ year journey with bipolar disorder, I have embraced my diagnosis and also realized that I am more than the sum total of a label. I learned above all, Hakeem Rahim is composed of experiences, loving relationships, passionate pursuits, creative endeavors.

In 2012, I began openly sharing my 14 year journey with bipolar disorder. My speaking and advocacy work has reached thousands of people including individuals living with mental illness and their family members. I also share my story with college, high school and middle school students to help teens and young adults combat stigma and transform the way they think about mental illness. Since January 2013, I have spoken at more than 50 educational institutions across the country.

I see the importance in and will continue to speak up for mental health and mental illness education in schools and beyond. I pray this creative endeavor serves as an affirmation that we are more than singular experiences, but rather individual, dynamic and powerful expressions motivation, faith, perseverance, confidence, love and hope.

Hakeem Rahim, Ed.M., M.A.

Hakeem Rahim, Ed.M, M.A. had the distinct honor of being the first African-American male valedictorian in his high school's history. He went on to graduate with a BA in psychology from Harvard University, and dual masters from Teacher's College, Columbia University.

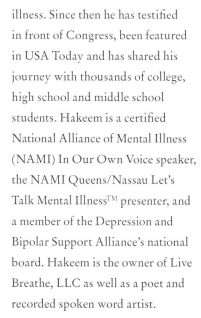

In 2012, Hakeem became an advocate for issues around mental illness. Since then he has testified in front of Congress, been featured in USA Today and has shared his journey with thousands of college, high school and middle school students. Hakeem is a certified National Alliance of Mental Illness (NAMI) In Our Own Voice speaker, the NAMI Queens/Nassau Let's Talk Mental Illness™ presenter, and a member of the Depression and Bipolar Support Alliance's national board. Hakeem is the owner of Live Breathe, LLC as well as a poet and recorded spoken word artist.

To find out more about booking Hakeem for presentations, keynotes and workshops please visit HakeemRahim.com.

CREDITS

Book Design: Elizabeth Hildebrandt, Section Photographs by Elizabeth & Charles Hildebrandt, Portrait by Petronella Photography

Made in the USA
Middletown, DE
12 July 2016